# Organization

## *The Top 100 Best Ways To Organize Your Life So That You Can Be More Productive, Efficient & At The Top Of Your Game*

By Ace McCloud
Copyright © 2014

# Disclaimer

The information provided in this book is designed to provide helpful information on the subjects discussed. This book is not meant to be used, nor should it be used, to diagnose or treat any medical condition. For diagnosis or treatment of any medical problem, consult your own physician. The publisher and author are not responsible for any specific health or allergy needs that may require medical supervision and are not liable for any damages or negative consequences from any treatment, action, application or preparation, to any person reading or following the information in this book. Any references included are provided for informational purposes only. Readers should be aware that any websites or links listed in this book may change.

# Table of Contents

Introduction ..................................................................... 6
Chapter 1: Organizing Your Home ............................... 8
Chapter 2: Organizing Your Digital Life ..................... 13
Chapter 3: Organizing Your Mind ............................... 15
Chapter 4: Organizing Your Relationships ................. 18
Chapter 5: Organizing Your Schedule ........................ 21
Chapter 6: Organizing Your Diet ................................ 23
Chapter 7: Organizing Your Budget ........................... 25
Chapter 8: A Well Rounded Organized Life ............... 28
Conclusion ................................................................. 30
My Other Books and Audio Books ............................ 31

**Be sure to check out my website for all my Books and Audio books.**

**www.AcesEbooks.com**

# Introduction

I want to thank you and congratulate you for buying the book: "Organization: The Top 100 Best Ways To Organize Your Life So That You Can Be More Productive, Efficient & At The Top Of Your Game"

This book contains proven steps and strategies on how to organize every part of your life!

We've all dealt with the perils of disorganization. You wake up late, slip on piles of unwashed clothes on the way to the shower, scramble to stuff an unhealthy breakfast in your mouth and still manage to be late for work. Your brain feels cluttered and it affects not only your mood but the moods of those around you. You may feel like you are always giving excuses for one mishap after another due to the disorganization problems that have piled up.

A disorganized life, in any capacity, can feel like a much larger burden of stress than it should. You feel tired, overwhelmed and unhappy with yourself. It can be more difficult to focus on goals that you want to accomplish or positive interactions with the ones that you love. Disorganization can lead to many health complications, which are easily avoidable. Surprised? Disorganization can take on the same attributes as chronic anxiety, eating away at you day after day. It's a shock to many that something as small as keeping a standardized to-do list can help you avoid stress-related illnesses, strokes and heart attacks. Unfortunately, disorganization is more of a disease than we think.

Organization affects many more parts of your life than you may assume. It can seem like a difficult beast to tackle, but if you're able to take a brief step back, decide what's most important to you in your life and make the conscious decisions every day to make these a priority; then you're well on your way to being far more organized and living much more happily and efficiently.

According to the Dictionary, it's the process of forming interdependent or coordinated parts, especially for united action. It's systemizing, giving organic structure to, and most importantly—it's the art of putting oneself in a state of mental competence to perform a task.

I'm sure all of these describe a much more transcendent place in life for many of you. It's a place where you don't need to worry about paying for dinner because all of your bills are paid and you know exactly how much money is left in the bank. With life moving more and more quickly every day, many don't take the time to think things through. Luckily there are hundreds of strategies and tools that you can utilize to stay more organized and be in control of your life.

Organization is a pathway to a happier, healthier you. When your life is in order, you feel far more empowered to try new things, meet new people and step outside of your comfort zone. You have so much less to worry about and you can focus on the parts of your life that matter the most.

Consider this your guide to the ultimate organization of your life. We'll focus on basic life organization along with home, schedule, relationships, diet, mind and budget organization. In this book you'll discover more than 100 tips and strategies to stay organized. You'll learn about how high impulsivity and disorganization can lead to weight gain and other negative things, you'll learn about helpful online tools to create budgets which can greatly help you financially, you'll also find great tips for meal prep and most of all, you'll learn how these all relate together to put you on the road to a happier, more fulfilled life.

Fun fact: It takes 21 days of repetitive activity for your body and mind to form a habit. Keep this in mind as you read on. If you integrate your favorite practices into your day-to-day routine and keep at it, you'll find being organized a breeze. By utilizing the tips and strategies in this book you will find that you have a cleaner space to work in, both physically and mentally, which will allow you to feel more motivated and inspired with far less stress and much more energy to go out and conquer the world!

# Chapter 1: Organizing Your Home

It's often said that the best way to stay functional, healthy and happy is to have a nice environment around you. Where does each day begin and end? Your home. What do most people end up spending most of their salary on? Their homes. Your home is the catalyst for how each day will transpire. Are you going to spring board from a place of tranquility and inspiration into your day? Or does the very act of being in your house already stress you out?

**Your Bedroom**

Let's start with your bedroom. Here are some tips to help keep everything in order:

1. **Wash your sheets weekly.** Sheets breed germs. There's probably some semblance of drool on your sheets and pillowcases, and honestly, they just smell better when freshly washed. Have trouble falling asleep at night? Wash your sheets with lavender infused detergent. It will help your mind start to slow down as soon as your head hits the pillow.

2. **Dust weekly.** Everything. This means blinds, furniture, floors and décor. One of the largest causes of allergies year-round is the dander and dust that you find in your own home. No need to get down on your hands and knees or slave with a mop, there's an abundance of technological advances which make keeping your floors clean very easy.

3. **Choose soothing colors for your surroundings.** This doesn't mean rushing out and buying a whole new set of furniture. It can be as simple as a throw blanket in your favorite color, or picture frames next to your bed in earthy greens. If you have a mind cluttered with to-dos already, steer clear of conflicting patterns and loud colors, which may contribute to stress headaches. Here's a tutorial that can help you choose appropriate paint colors for different living spaces.

4. **Listen to soothing music before you go to bed.** Again, there's no correct genre for this. Although hard metal may not be the best option, I've found that a sleepy time playlist with some of my favorite slow-paced songs helps lull me to slumber even before the playlist has finished. If your mind won't stop spinning, try recording positive mantras or even your to-do list for the next day to listen to before bed and get yourself in the right frame of mind to fall asleep.

## Your Bathroom

Now on to the bathroom. Surprisingly, a well-organized bathroom will speed up your morning routine and make getting ready for bed much easier. If you don't have a morning routine, develop one. Sit down and make a checklist of your health and beauty to-dos that you'd like to accomplish. These may include-

- Showering

- Washing/conditioning your hair

- Washing your face

- Brushing your teeth

- Shaving

- Developing a morning ritual is also super important and something peak performers due every morning. Some more ideas include reciting positive affirmations, stretching, listening to positive and uplifting music, going over your goals, eating something healthy, watching uplifting videos, deep breathing, yoga, a quick exercise routine and anything else that will help you start the day in a positive and uplifting way! It's said that people who avoid checking their email for more than an hour after waking up are 30% more productive during the day! Get your mornings started right and you may be shocked at just how good the rest of the day will go!

Remove the more time-intensive parts of your beauty routine and save those for the weekend. Here are some [time saving tips you may find helpful.](#) Many women find that saving activities like deep-conditioning masques, facials and nail treatments for the weekends, make them look forward to them a lot more, also encouraging them to complete them more regularly.

Now that you've streamlined your beauty routine, ensure that your products, tools and anything else that you may need to get ready in the morning are all accessible and neatly organized. Your brain may be foggy when you first awake and you want to create an autopilot routine for you to complete.

Space is often a challenge in bathrooms, especially with so many products to keep track of. Here is a great YouTube video with tips on [How to Organize Your Bathroom](#) by The Lindquists.

It's also very important to ensure that your bathroom is clean. Dirt is one of the top contributors to stress that is related to disorganization. Germs in your bathroom can also cause sickness, especially if you're sharing a bathroom with family members or friends. Clean all surfaces at least once weekly and try to give your bath or shower an intensive clean at least once a month.

The bathroom and the kitchen are probably the rooms where you keep the most products. Keep a list of products that you keep stocked and mark them down on a list when you know you're getting low and when you're completely out. If you keep these lists on a digital device, sync them with your shopping list, so that you can make sure you pick up everything that you need when running errands.

**Your Kitchen**

Time to move on to the kitchen. The kitchen can be daunting to organize, as it's often a gathering place for family and friends as well as the hub of your meals. Let's start with meal prep.

Meal prep has become an increasing trend for parents and professionals alike. Set aside an hour one day during the week to shop and prepare meals for the whole week. Looking for a healthy option? Make a massive batch of salad or whole grain pasta with whatever fixings you prefer. If you really want to be healthy then don't add dressing. Divide salads into different plastic bins for each day of the week and then add any wet ingredients or dressing before leaving for work or school.

Sandwiches are also a good option. People around the world spend thousands of dollars each year dining out on expensive lunches. There is a tremendous variety of cheeses, meats, veggies and bread that you can choose from very inexpensively? In general, making your own lunch can save you around $780 per year. Put that money into a savings account and watch it add up.

Meal prep will save you valuable money and time and it doesn't stop at lunch. Take a little additional time each Sunday to plan family dinners for the week. Mapping these out will make trips to the grocery store much more time effective. You can buy in bulk the ingredients that you know you'll be using multiple times to save money.

**Bonus tip:** Grocery shop smarter. Remember that perishables are always placed around the perimeter of your grocery store or supermarket, with dry goods in the center aisles. Walk the perimeter of the store to cross off those items, before exploring the aisles. Remember to not grocery shop hungry or you will tend to buy more things that you may not need, especially sugary and tasty snacks.

Once you've finished your grocery shopping, it's time to put everything away. Make sure that you have easy accessibility to the items that you use the most.

Keep the healthier items in your line of sight and pack the guilty pleasure items further out of reach or hidden in a cabinet. You're still allowed to enjoy them; you just won't be tempted by them every time you walk in the kitchen.

The kitchen is another room where space can be an issue. Here is a helpful YouTube resource with more [tips for storage](.).

It never hurts to keep track of use-by dates either. Make sure that you're consuming your groceries in a timely manner so that you're not throwing food and money in the trash. If you think you might forget, make notes on your grocery list so you can keep track of what you may need to pick up more often.

Your fridge can easily become a multipurpose organizational tool. Consider it a chalkboard for your life. Since it's a place that you frequent, it's a helpful canvas for to-do lists, shopping lists, reminders for family members or even positive mantras to help you seize the day. That being said, it's easy to let it fall into disarray, covered by (amazing) drawings by the kids and photos of friends and family. Keep an area for these mementoes, but give some space for reminders as well. Also be sure to keep your refrigerator clean and organized. Throw away old items and put the most commonly used items in easy to reach places. It's also a good idea to keep the fruits and vegetables within easy reach if you are looking to live a [healthy](.) and energy filled life.

**Common Living Areas**

Any room with a television in it is going to be a popular one. In an age that's increasingly growing more digital, people of all ages turn to electronic media to unwind after a day at work. It's important to give these spaces a little extra love so that they're inviting for hobbies of all kinds, not just a home for whatever entertainment system you have.

Where you may have chosen soothing colors for your bedroom, pick cheery colors for the living room. It's the perfect opportunity to share your style with decorative touches. Exercising your [creative](.) side actually contributes to organization as it allows you a stress release, bringing your brain back to a focused place.

Ensure that there's enough seating for visitors, so that everyone isn't crammed in a corner. Fung Shui teaches the art of angling items in your living spaces to capitalize on positive energy opportunities. If it's something you're interested in learning about, check out this YouTube video by Rodika Tchi: [How To Apply Feng Shui In 3 Easy Steps](.). At base level it's also common sense to have everything in the room facing the center, so that there's more room for entertaining.

Again, not a fan of dust? Keep the living spaces tidy with cabinets and organizers for toys, trinkets and movies. You can also alphabetize your movies so that you know exactly where to find the perfect one right when you're looking for it.

We've covered the basic rooms of the house. Here are some takeaways-

- Avoid dust with weekly cleanings, keeping you and loved ones happy and sniffle free.

- Keep inventory of your beauty products and put together a morning and evening routine.

- Take some time once a week to plan your grocery shopping and meals for the week. Shop smart, and never hungry.

- Choose surroundings that soothe and empower you. Avoid jarring patterns.

Bottom line; make the time in your schedule to plan for an organized home. If you make the time, sit down and make a plan, you're already on your way to an organized home. If you still find that you are overwhelmed with things, be sure to organize your closets and sell off everything that you don't need! You may be shocked at just how good you can feel when you give away, throw away, or sell all that extra stuff that you never use anymore! **This concept is called minimalism and it is one of the most important things you can do to live a more organized life!** Check out this YouTube video to help get yourself motivated and ready for an organized and clutter free life: How To Become A Minimalist Danny Dover.

# Chapter 2: Organizing Your Digital Life

We live in a digital age where your technology can be your biggest tool in becoming more organized. Many people have put their entire lives on devices like tablets, smart phones and computers. Most every part of many people's lives can be connected to the Internet. This can be a blessing and a curse. It can aid in balancing work and personal life, but sometimes it just becomes stressful and inconvenient. Here are a few tips and strategies to put your digital world in order.

**Keep each project's content in one place**
If you're working on a multimedia project—photos, spreadsheets, word documents etc., have them all organized in their own special place. One good idea is to save each media type in one general or master folder so that it is much easier to navigate through everything quickly and easily. This can save you time from bouncing from one place on the computer to the next trying to track down different things.

**Make sure your files are always accessible**
Whether it's your boss asking for a recent report or your daughter asking you to send her math homework to her, sometimes your digital data is saved on a variety of different devices. Take advantage of software programs like iCloud, Google Drive or Dropbox to ensure that all data is saved in a central location. I personally just started using Dropbox and love it! I also would recommend an external hard drive which is very easy to back up important documents on as well. Looking for a more intensive solution? Set up a NAS (network-attached solution). NAS Providers use iOS and Android apps that allow you to access all of your files through your smart phone.

**Use tags to organize and find your photos**
After you move your photos to your computer from your camera or phone, take a few minutes to organize them with tags. Several tools that can help with this include QNAP's Photo Station and Google Picasa. Some can even recognize faces, which speeds the process up even more. Once your photos are tagged, you can search for them on your computer just like any other file type. Otherwise, you can organize pictures using folders. I personally have folders for my favorite pictures, A folder for the pictures I use most often, then the other folders organized by date. There are a variety of great programs that will allow you to organize your photo collection very easily.

**Back up regularly**
It can't be said enough, every piece of digital content you've ever created can be gone in a second. Put together a regular backup routine, copying all files to an external hard drive or cloud based software. I like to group all my files in one place by "personal" and "business." I can then easily highlight these areas and then save them to an external hard drive quite easily.

**Digitize music to clear up space**
If you were around before the age of iTunes, chances are you have other forms of music lying around the house, probably collecting dust. The time has come for you to digitize these files and store away the CDs or records. Insert CDs into your computer drive and copy all files to your server or computer. Make sure that they're properly labeled so that they're easy to find. If you are hanging on to older records, the process may be a little bit more time consuming, but just as worth it. Then you can also put the cd's into organizing cases which can hold hundreds of discs in the space of a large book. Another great idea is to make song lists from your favorite music. I currently have about 8 different song lists that each holds my favorite music of all time. Once you have this organized, just simply go back to them again and again more sheer joy and enjoyment! Then just continue to create more personalized lists as you find more and more music. The time spent organizing your music will pay huge dividends in the long run! I have personally found that windows media player is the best way to organize music. There is a download that you can buy that will also allow you to synchronize your windows media player with your iPod. It is called MGTEK. ITunes has pissed me off so bad in the past in the limits they have on organizing music that I try to do everything from windows media player now, which is much more user friendly!

**Save your business cards**
Business cards are far from irrelevant, but they can easily get lost in the clutter of your wallet or organizer. Save them in your phone as contacts. A good program for this is Google Goggles. These can be saved in their own contact group, so they don't clutter personal contacts. When you want to forward their contact info, just send the digital content via message or email.

**OneNote or EverNote**
I can't recommend getting a program like OneNote or EverNote enough! A friend told me about OneNote 16 months ago and I ignored her advice for about four months. I finally got around to looking into it and all I can say is: "**WOW!**" This program has been life changing. I have been using it for the last year and I have my life set up like a peak performance mastermind genius! If used properly, you can organize so much on there! Some of the incredible features of OneNote is that it automatically saves things instantly, you can put links to websites and YouTube videos in there, you can easily create a digital journal just by organizing entries according to month, you can have a whole section dedicated to personal and a whole section dedicated to business, and then further divide those groups into all the different aspects that you want to have super quick and easy access to. I put everything on OneNote and then make sure that the backup of the file is in an easy to access folder which can then be easily backed up online or on an external hard drive. I would highly recommend a program like this for you in which you can easily organize almost every aspect of your digital life.

Follow these simple digital hacks and soon you'll find your time and space online are easier to navigate and far less stressful.

# Chapter 3: Organizing Your Mind

Organization goes above and beyond the tangible aspects of your life, which you can see. It isn't just about de-cluttering your house or office; it isn't just about the latest gadget or technology. An organized mind enables an engaged lifestyle.

The mind's ability to reach a calm and positive place is the biggest tool to be wise and strategic in how you plan out not only your day-to-day life, but also the [goals](#) on the horizon that you wish to achieve.

Recently neuroscientists are opening many windows into disorganized minds, specifically those with attention affecting disorders (ADHD, ADD, etc.). Based on this research, they're able to offer many insights on ways we can train our brains to be more organized.

According to the National Institute of Aging, many of the symptoms of a disorganized mind correlate with higher weight. These include chronic negativity, impulsivity, high stress and multitasking. Interestingly enough, the top 10% of those showing signs of high impulsivity weighed about 25 lbs more than those who were in the bottom 10%. The takeaway is that, if you're able to keep your attention focused under pressure, you're able to "drive" your attention and hyper focus your organization much more easily.

Here are some tips to keep your mind in a "driven" place-

1. **Identify your stress and tame it-** It's impossible to focus your attention if negative stress factors are dominating your mind. These include worry, sadness, fear, irritation, personal problems, frustration, etc. Luckily, the same strategies to keep your body in shape will also help work out your mind and keep you in a positive place. Exercise regularly, sleep well and remember to breathe deeply and to stop and smell the roses whenever you feel that life is moving too quickly. This can be easier said than done, as many of you already know. For more advanced help on eliminating stress and forgiving the pains of the past, feel free to check out my books: [Forgiveness](#) and [Overcoming Fear](#). I would also recommend checking out the variety of free "Tapping" videos on YouTube as they can be quite helpful.

2. **Laser your focus-** Your brain is not built to multitask. It's meant to do one task at a time, and when in the proper frame of mind, it does it well. Embrace one task at a time, and only allow anything to do with that task to engage you. Turn off distractions (social media, phone, background noise) and try to spend 10 minutes only focusing on the task at hand. Once you've gotten the hang of it, increase time periods blocked off. Remember to give yourself sporadic breaks so that your mind doesn't wander. This is something all the peak performers in the world do! Some things that have helped me include the supplement [Focus Formula](#) and this is a great

YouTube video that can enhance your concentration: Creative Focus by Jason Lewis. Remember to use the famous 80/20 rule to decide what you should be focusing on! You should be focusing on the 20% of activities that yield 80% of the best results!

3. **"Shift Sets"-** Once you've mastered the process of focusing on one skill, try what many scientists call a "Shift Set". This is basically moving your full attention from one task to the next. Scientists also call this cognitive agility or flexibility. It's been found that some of the most famous creative ideas have come during shift sets, when you shift to using a completely different part of your brain.

4. **Create a "Launch Pad" for your belongings-** As far as the tangible necessities of your day-to-day life go, create a launch pad at the start of every day. This will be a place where you can put everything needed for the next day. This way you'll always know where they are and they will be quickly accessible. Create one launch pad at home and one at work. Make sure that your necessities always make it to this spot at the end of the day.

5. **Designate appropriate time for projects-** Some projects will take weeks of your life. Others, just a few minutes. Don't switch back and forth between the two. Block out adequate time blocks for both so that your focus isn't strained. Be sure to bunch appropriate tasks together to save time in the long run. It is much easier to prepare five lunches ahead of time than it is to make one lunch per day. This is a huge key to being more productive and organized! Be sure to bunch similar tasks together then focus on that one task until it is completed. This skill has made a huge difference in my personal productivity!

6. **Don't spend more time on a decision than you have to-** Figure out how important a decision is to you and what impact it will have on those around you. Your time is valuable. Often times it is much more valuable to make a decision quickly than to make delays. Even if you make a wrong decision, you will have more time to learn from your mistake and move forward smarter and wiser. The best leaders in the world make decisions in a time sensitive manner.

7. **Leave work at work-** When you're at work, be fully at work. When you're able to leave and go home, do it! This is your time to recharge and come back to work the next day driven and with a purpose. Without life balance you'll lose your drive to succeed in the office and spread yourself too thin.

8. **Hypnosis-** I am a huge fan of audio hypnosis and have been using it for years with great success! I personally think the best place in the world to get this material is at: HypnosisDownloads.com. I have at least fifty of their hypnosis downloads and a few of my favorites are Focus and

Concentration and with Forgive and Move On. The nice thing about this website is you can download the audios instantly and they are total pro's at what they do.

9. [Meditation](#) and [Yoga](#) are well known for their mental benefits and highly recommended!

The important, abstract aspects of our lives can be easier to manage with life hacks. Hopefully the tips above will help lead you to a clearer mind, which can focus and also equally importantly, let go. One of the biggest qualifiers for stress is over analyzing. It's tough to follow through on, but the more you can put everything into perspective, the more you'll be able to believe that that bad conversation or project, which didn't have the outcome you hoped to achieve, is really small in the greater scheme of your life. Remember the greatest people in life tend to be those who can overcome failures or disappointments over and over again until they inevitably succeed.

Organizing your mind will probably be the longest leg of your journey on your road to organization. This is a good thing. Hopefully it will continue throughout your life as you hone your decision making process, clear your mind, and discover what's most important to you in your life. Just like your body will get weak without exercise, so will your mind. So make it a [habit](#) to be mentally powerful! Just remember that you are the only one in control of the organization of your mind and that it starts with just one deep breath.

# Chapter 4: Organizing Your Relationships

Organizing and prioritizing your relationships can be extremely difficult because you're bringing feelings and emotions into the mix. However, it's important to take into account who brings what into your life. Do you have any positive mentors helping you? Are you lucky enough to have an inspirational manager at your job? Got people in your life who are just a joy to be around? If yes, be sure to work time with them into your schedule and make an extra effort to be friends with them. Family and close friends who are supportive of you should be integrated into your schedule regularly, to nourish and nurture your overall wellbeing. But the first step in organizing your relationships is eliminating anyone who brings negative energy into your life. These people are monopolizing the time that you can be spending doing things you enjoy with positive, uplifting people.

There are several kinds of friends that are vital to keep around-

**The Mom-** This friend will keep your decision-making skills in check, a handy person to have around if you're aiming to become more organized. They won't be your craziest comrades, but they'll offer sage advice whether you want to hear it or not.

**The Cheerleader-** The cheerleader will be your biggest fan. Whenever you need a pick-me-up, they'll be there for support. The cheerleader and mom are great friends to have in tandem if you're feeling down or having a rough day.

**The Lifer-** This friend has been there since day one. They know your good traits and bad ones and love them all equally. They're potentially your most objective friends because they know you so well. They're allowed the privilege of tough love, and it's likely you're able to give it right back to them.

**The fearless adventurer-** This friend is an asset for personal advancement. With their help, you push yourself beyond what you know you're capable of. They're always the first one to suggest a spontaneous trip, staying out all night with people you've never met before and following through on the things you're too scared to do. Keep them around because they'll help you create an arsenal of irreplaceable memories.

**The mentor-** This friend is a bit of a hybrid—intelligent, driven and often older and/or more mature than you. Find as many mentors as you can in your life. They can offer priceless advice in both your personal life and your professional life. Remember to heed their advice. They don't have to give it to you. They're giving it to you out of the goodness of their hearts. You can also have a mentor anytime you want by buying a great book or course from the many great choice out there. Two of my favorite mentors are Tony Robbins and Arnold Schwarzenegger. Here are a couple of very insightful bonus videos from each of these great men: The Six Secrets to Success posted by Travis Fisher and Money: Master The Game posted by Marie Forleo.

**The Opposites Attract Friend-** although you'll often want to bite their head off, the opposites attract friend may be the best friend of all when it comes to staying organized. We're wired as human beings to stick together in groups or packs, and attack outsiders. However, if you only become friends with like-minded individuals, you'll maintain the same habits and you'll never grow. Breaking out of your comfort zone is an important part of becoming organized; you're breaking the habits that you've grown accustomed to. You'll have your eyes opened to different views and become more accepting of those around you.

Try and identify a friend in your life who falls into each description. They'll be important in your journey to organization.

Similarly, there are several kinds of friends or people in your life who will hinder this progress-

**The Jealous Friend-** Not to be mistaken for The Competitive Friend, The Jealous Friend has a way of making you feel bad about all of your achievements. They'll try to monopolize the majority of your energy instead of helping you focus it towards your own goals. Unfortunately, competition is a trait seen in many driven professionals. Make sure that you align yourself with those who push you competitively but who also celebrate your success.

**The Flaky Friend-** We have all had one. And most of the time we love him or her, but a flaky friend can be the most dangerous weapon in your battle to stay organized. They have zero time efficiency skills, which frequently can mean that they dominate your time without realizing it. These friends are far more focused on their own priorities and cannot be counted on for support or consistently valuable advice. If you want to have any chance at being one of the best in the world, or at the very least happy and efficient, eliminate the negative impact of these types of people as much as possible. Remember that your time and energy is very important, and if someone is consistently wasting it, then spend your time trying to find someone else who isn't going to annoy you and hold you back!

**The Untrustworthy Friend-** Unfortunately this friend can be tough to spot, but it's vital that you do. An untrustworthy friend can intrude on many aspects of your life, be it relationships, your home, your job or your belongings. Untrustworthy friends frequently put up the best fronts and end up disappointing you. They also tend to be very good liars and will say almost anything to try and regain your trust after betraying you. They may be very charming and quite used to backstabbing people then talking their way out of it. Stay on course by spending time with friends you can trust professionally and personally and eliminating those who are using you for their own ends.

Now you know the important types of people to spend time with and those to avoid as you're trying to organize your personal relationships. This should eliminate a lot of stress around your relationship organization. Remember, to be the best you need to hang around the best. If you hang out with losers and negative people then it is going to be much harder for you to have a happy and productive life!

The next step is ensuring you're the kind of friend that people want to spend time with, and that you consistently follow through with plans. Your schedule is an important organizational tool and spending time with friends and loved ones should very present on it. You can also try and get an accountability partner who you can share your goals and dreams with, who will keep you accountable and also motivate you towards success. You can also hire a life coach who can help you towards achieving your goals or you can join a mastermind group or other positive and uplifting group that focuses on success and the more positive things in life. I personally have been performing much better after finding a great accountability partner and joining an elite mastermind group. There are a lot of great Facebook groups out there where you can search for some great and uplifting online friends.

It's also important to work "me-time" into the balance. Statistics have shown that a healthy balance of work – family – friends - me time have led to the happiest individuals. It's up to you how you spend this time. You can be as indulgent as you want, or as productive as you want. It's a time that no one else can intrude on. It's up to you how much of it you put your time and energy towards. I personally like to do a morning routine and an evening routine and have had tremendous success with these... especially the morning routine!

# Chapter 5: Organizing Your Schedule

This leads me to the next element of organization... your schedule. You have seven days in the week but it may frequently feel like you need two or three more days to accomplish everything on your to-do list. In each section of this book, I've touched on finding time to organize that element of your life. Time is something that many people feel like they don't have. Stop, pause and remind yourself to not think that way.

Can't seem to shake the anxiety around your valuable time? Think of someone whose achievements or accomplishments you admire. They have the exact same amount of time in a week that you do. If they can do it, then so can you.

Pick a day, any day that you will set aside time to organize all elements of your life. This means making shopping lists, to do lists, keeping your house in order, budgeting frugally for said lists, calling friends you haven't seen in a while, making plans for the week and taking some time to reflect on what you've accomplished over the last seven days. The last part is particularly important. In order to feel enthused and motivated to make a plan for the week ahead, it's nice to stop and think about what you've achieved.

For many, Sunday is the best day for this as it helps you get a jump-start on the week ahead. Here is a good checklist to work off of, so that you can go to bed on Sunday feeling like you're ready to conquer the week-

1. **Finish Meal Plan-** Brainstorm meals that save well for the nights you don't feel up to cooking or don't have time.

2. **Create Shopping List-** Break it down by food groups, keeping in mind the layout of the grocery store and how perishable each item on your list is. This will give you better visuals of what exactly you need to stock up on each week.

3. **Weekly Budget Complete-** It's very important to stick within this budget. This will take some trial and error so don't be too hard on yourself, but once you've tried meal planning a few weeks in a row, you will figure out exactly what you can afford on your budget.

4. **Complete Weekly Shopping-** Find a superstore near you that will accommodate as many of your errand needs as possible. If you prefer to shop at smaller, local grocery shops, that's great! Just budget a little bit more time for you to finish everything.

5. **Miscellaneous Errands-** This can cover everything from laundry to mail and other miscellaneous errands in between. As I mentioned above, try and condense these into as few stops as possible. This will save on gas and help your sanity. Bring a checklist for errand stops and everything

you need to buy at each one so that you know that you won't forget anything.

6. **Weekly activity budget set-** Frugality is important, but so is creating lasting memories. Encourage yourself to spend time out of the house, just make sure that you're keeping your budget in mind when making your plans. Instead of meeting friends at happy hours and fancy dinners five nights a week, plan a once a week get together with a group of friends where you can rotate that hosts. This is a good way to combine your groups of friends, meet new people and not be too stressed about money.

7. *Now relax and enjoy your evening, knowing that you're ready to seize the week! Think of all the things you are grateful for and give yourself a pat on the back.*

# Chapter 6: Organizing Your Diet

Organizing your diet isn't just about keeping a shape that you're proud of. Organizing your diet allows you to live a longer, healthier life. Your skin will think you; your teeth and nails will thank you, your energy levels with thank you and every part of your body benefits from a well-organized diet.

Healthy eating can be challenging enough, but a lack of a strategic approach can make you feel scattered and discouraged. If you don't learn self-discipline and the willingness to step outside the box, you can find yourself in a whole world of hurt and problems.

Thinking this might be your largest area of struggle? Here are some tips to maintain healthy habits and achieve diet organization success. A lot of these we've covered in past sections, but it's worth another reminder that organizing each area of your life sets you up for more and more success.

1. **Have a Plan-** As we discussed, meal prep is crucial for success in organization. Above and beyond meal ideas for the week, brainstorm healthy, filling snacks. Without meal prep, you're going to be more likely to make impulse decisions at the drive through, spending unnecessary money and increasing calories and cholesterol.

2. **Get rid of food that's not in your plan-** If it's not included in your meals and snacks for the week, it has to go. Have a clean, fresh start. It's important to de-clutter the kitchen to avoid temptation and stay driven to success. If you live with a roommate, or a family member with special dietary needs, discuss a designated area for your food and theirs.

3. **Make the time to shop and make time to prepare food-** It's a good idea to set aside time a few times per week, you only need an hour or so. During this time chop and peel your vegetables. If you need to marinate any meat, prepare that marinade and let your meats sit. Ensure that your fruit is freshly washed and ready to be used.

4. **Organize your kitchen-** Keep all utensils and tools you need in preparing healthy meals close at hand. Choose a particular cupboard where you can store commonly used spices, measuring cups and spoons, menu ideas, a scale for food and other tools that you'll need to keep handy.

**Bonus Tip-** Keep a recipe stash that you can contribute to, over time. There are tons and tons of resources on the Web for fun and healthy recipes to try. Pinterest is a great place to get started for visuals of what looks like a delicious and nutritious meal for you. Reach out to your friends for their favorite recipes. This ensures that your meal planning will stay dynamic, never becoming too monotonous or boring. If you are looking for easy to make, inexpensive, healthy and energizing recipes then be sure to check out my books: Gluten Free Recipes, Recipe Book and Vegetarian Diet Recipes.

It's also important to utilize your freezer. A well-stocked and organized freezer can be the organized cook's best friend. Knowing which foods to buy in bulk and freeze will save you lots of money and time.

Remember that just because you buy foods in bulk, if you don't freeze them properly, they won't do you any good. Purchase plastic Tupperware, heavy-duty aluminum wrap and shrink plastic bags for storage.

Freeze meals in the portion sizes you think that you'll use on a regular basis. Also, if only one member of your household loves a particular dish, freeze it in single servings instead of a large batch. This way, it's easy to take one serving out and prepare it without thawing the entire dish.

# Chapter 7: Organizing Your Budget

A disorganized budget can easily contribute to stress in other areas of your life. An organized budget helps you sort out priorities in your life and where to spend your hard earned dollars. When you monitor your budget regularly, you'll be able to figure out exactly where you're spending your money and how to tweak your budget as needed.

Similarly, when you're trying to get out of debt and/or take control of your financial big picture, it's an absolute necessity to begin with a budget. By following a budget, you you control your money so you can reach your financial goals.

A popular introduction to budgeting is the 50-30-20 plan. This system allocates fifty percent of your earnings to living expenses. This includes mortgage or rent payments, transportation costs, food and utilities. Thirty percent should be set aside for savings and payments. This includes credit card payments, car payments and savings for a rainy day. The remaining twenty percent can be spent on what I like to refer to as lifestyle expenses. This covers dining out, shopping, excursions and adventures. If you stick to this plan, you're already on your way to creating a solid framework.

Let's dive into this a little deeper, starting with living expenses. It's important to not live beyond your means. Especially with younger generations, don't assume you'll be able to afford your dream home immediately out of college. If you continue to save for a rainy day, you'll have much more to look forward to when you're established in life. If you're not careful, you can easily end up with thousands of dollars of credit card and other debt which can cost hundreds of dollars per month in just interest alone!

Living costs will adjust city to city, so be realistic with what you can afford. If spending time out on the town or frequent travel is important to you, you may have to live in a smaller home. Again, it's all about priorities. You can also research better areas to live. If you live near a major city, you may only be able to afford a small house, but if you live in a suburb, you may be able to live in a large house for the same amount of money.

Create goals for your savings. These can be exciting trips, expensive clothing, or something else that will incentivize you to set money aside. It's helpful to keep this money in a separate bank account. Some banks even have settings that don't allow you to touch your money for extended periods of time. Choose banks with higher return rates, so that it will grow over time.

Looking for ways to kick-start your savings habit? Here are some easy places to cut spending-

1. **Your tax refund.** Whether you're expecting it or not, put your refund aside in savings when you receive.

2. **Surprise bonuses and raises**. Again, you're probably not expecting this increase in cash. If you save it, you're encouraging yourself to live within your means.

3. **Sell your belongings that you don't need anymore.** Outdated CD's, old furniture, clothes, books and other items that are cluttering up your living space. Sites like eBay; Craigslist and many local Websites offer easy to use services to pay you for stuff lying around your house. Some will even pick these items up if you are giving them away. The return may not be huge, but the fact that you're getting paid to clean your own house? Well worth the time. Bonus? A cleaner house and better mental wellbeing.

Your twenty percent for lifestyle expenses should not intrude into the other areas of your budget. This is money that you can use to reward yourself for saving well. It doesn't hurt to keep this money in a separate savings account as well. This way you can watch it grow and feel more and more inspired to save it, rather than waste it on frivolous expenses. It's very important to acknowledge this part of your budget in financial planning. With the reminder that you do have money to spend on short-term needs that make you happy, those that focus 100% of their energy on savings and paying bills are more likely to be stressed and then break down and make an unwise decision/purchase.

Some people work best documenting their budget on paper. For these folks, remember to keep track of all purchases. Bonus points for saving receipts. These are important for end of year tax documentation as well as to ensure that there are never any discrepancies by retailers or service providers.

Alternatively, if you aren't partial to pen and paper, there are many tools on the Web to help you organize and maintain a healthy budget including great YouTube Resources. MakingLifeSimple offers invaluable advice for putting together a budget.

One Website resource worth checking out is Learnvest, a Website with articles, an easy-to-use budget creation processes and customer service resources that you can reach out to for help. Another Web based option to check out is called Mint. Mint will even send weekly updates of where exactly you're spending your money, in pie chart form. Both Mint, Learnvest and other budgeting tools offer mobile apps as well so you can check your progress before making that impulse purchase.

At the end of the day, as mentioned before, organizing one area of your life will quickly affect another. Budgeting properly will have a large influence on every area of your life. When you prioritize your spending, pay your bills on time and keep that piggy bank for a rainy day full, you'll feel encouraged to organize other areas of your life as well. For more advanced information feel free to check out my bestselling books: Making Money & Saving Money.

# Chapter 8: A Well Rounded Organized Life

As we've discussed, organizing your life is a multi-tiered process, but once you get the ball rolling, you'll be astounded at the progress that you make. Organizing your finances affects organizing your schedule which affects organizing your to-do list which affects organizing your finances, etc. Let's brainstorm the top ten takeaways that you can bring away from reading this book-

1. **Make the time-** Set aside some time each week to decompress and make your organizational plan for the days ahead. Taking advantage of this time will help you be fully equipped and prepared for the challenges of the week ahead and you'll go into Monday with a clear, focused mind.

2. **List it out-** Lists (digital or hand written) will be your mapping tool to full organization. Keep track of errands, which need to be run, groceries that need to be purchased, calls to be returned and to-dos, which need to be taken care of. Keep these lists in an easily accessible area of your phone, computer or notebook.

3. **Prep your meals-** Chop, can and store all ingredients for your lunches in the week to come. Freeze any ingredients you can in airtight containers and plastic bags so that they last longer. Buy ingredients in bulk whenever you can and use perishables in a timely manner before they go bad.

4. **Clean your house regularly-** A tidy house will encourage you to spend more time at home, instead of spending money going out. Keeping your house neat and clean will also encourage you to appreciate it more.

5. **Do a digital clean up-** Get rid of excess documents, emails, photos and music to open up space on your computer. Organize the ones you hold on to in specific folders that are easily accessible. Make sure that all assets are labeled correctly and easy to track down.

6. **Back up, back up, back up-** Make sure that you're backing up your computer data at least once a month, if not more. Use services like Google Drive or iCloud for free or purchase an external hard drive to back up on.

7. **Make financial goals-** Financial goals are the best incentive to keep more money in the bank. If you set feasible goals for yourself, you'll know exactly what you're working towards with your savings. Put this money in an account that you can't touch. Even if your savings goal is just for "rainy days ahead", you'll feel financially safe knowing that you're protecting your future self.

8. **Surround yourself with good friends-** If you spend your time with the right people, you'll feel encouraged to live a much more dynamic and

organized life. It might sound harsh, but cutting ties with people that are holding you back or putting you down is a great tool to organize your life.

9. **Don't spread yourself too thin-** you have 24 hours a day, 7 days a week. Use these to your maximum benefit. Sometimes this will mean saying no to happy hours or a friends request to hang out. You know what your goals and dreams are and what you need to do in order to accomplish them. It almost never comes easy and those who are the most disciplined and hardest working are usually the ones smiling with the trophy in their hand at the end.

10. **Breathe-** Everything is always fixable. Nothing is so urgent that you don't have time to stop and think things through. Remember to stop and think all of your actions through before acting.

Some of these will be more applicable to your life than others. Still struggling with getting started? Pick your top three to tackle in the coming weeks. Start with just one and try and integrate it into your daily life. Once you've gotten the hang of it, add another top-ten tip to your routine. Don't beat yourself up if you have off days, these are all part of the process. Over time you'll appreciate how much better you feel with these tips in your life. I can tell you that I personally have every area of my life expertly organized and it is truly amazing just how much more efficient, happy and productive you truly can be when everything is in its proper place!

# Conclusion

I hope this book was able to help you to organize every area of your life.

The next step is to find your incentive, dig deep into your determination and begin to take the steps necessary towards a well-rounded and organized life.

In my mind it's here that the journey starts, where the desire and inspiration to start your adventure to organization and life domination really begins. Once you have your life fully organized, then you may truly begin to see some incredible results and begin to realize just how powerful you can truly become.

Remember that even small changes can have an exponentially positive effect on your life and those around you. I can't emphasize enough how important it is to just take one small step towards organizing your life and then just never giving up on it! If you can start your day with just one small improvement to your daily routine, then you're already on your way.

Remember that everyone is different, there is no cookie cutter, guaranteed path that works for everyone. Are you a people person? Talk to those that you admire and learn their secrets. Prefer to research online or in books? There are a plethora of supplemental articles, programs and Websites that can enhance your learnings.

My most sincere wish is that I've given you many great ideas on how you can improve your life by organizing and given you the inspiration and motivation to move forward with your organizing efforts!

Being organized will make you that much more closer to being unstoppable in both your personal and professional life! Research has shown that organized people are exponentially more confident, happy and healthy.

Remember that this is not a magic journey that happens overnight. It will take grit and determination to make success happen. If you're feeling down, remember to breathe. Breathe and remember exactly why this is so important to you. Is it for a loved one? Is it for a promotion? Most of all, is it for you and your lifelong happiness? Feel these incentives cheering you on as you integrate more and more organizational habits into your routine and be sure to reward yourself for the many victories that are sure to come your way!

Finally, if you discovered at least one thing that has helped you or that you think would be beneficial to someone else, be sure to take a few seconds to easily post a quick positive review. As an author, your positive feedback is desperately needed. Your highly valuable five star reviews are like a river of golden joy flowing through a sunny forest of mighty trees and beautiful flowers! *To do your good deed in making the world a better place by helping others with your valuable insight, just leave a nice review.*

**My Other Books and Audio Books**
www.AcesEbooks.com

# Health Books

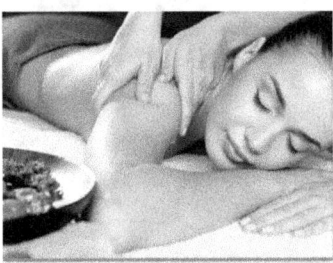

# Peak Performance Books

## Be sure to check out my audio books as well!

 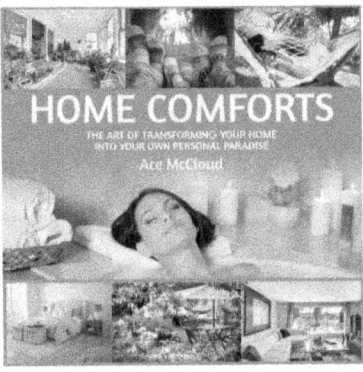 

Check out my website at: www.AcesEbooks.com for a complete list of all of my books and high quality audio books. I enjoy bringing you the best knowledge in the world and wish you the best in using this information to make your journey through life better and more enjoyable! **Best of luck to you!**

www.ingramcontent.com/pod-product-compliance
Lightning Source LLC
Chambersburg PA
CBHW051428070526
44584CB00023B/3629